I'm drawing a picture

a picture

doretta groenendyk

The Acorn Press
Charlottetown
2015

ACORNPRESS

P.O. Box 22024
Charlottetown, Prince Edward Island
C1A 9J2
acornpresscanada.com

Printed in Canada by Marquis
Edited by Penelope Jackson
Design by Matt Reid

Library and Archives Canada Cataloguing in Publication

Groenendyk, Doretta, author
I'm drawing a picture / Doretta Groenendyk.

ISBN 978-1-927502-50-1 (paperback)

1. Drawing--Juvenile literature. 2. Art--Juvenile literature.
I. Title.

NC655.G76 2015   j741.2   C2015-904412-X

The publisher acknowledges the support of the Government of Canada
through the Canada Book Fund of the Department of Canadian Heritage,
the Canada Council of the Arts Block Grant Program and the support
of the Province of Prince Edward Island.

for david, reilly,
izra and jasper

A lot can happen
when we create.
Join the fun—
what can YOU make?

I can sculpt a castle for you!

I'll build it as high as the sky
and as wide as the sea.

My handprints will wave to the water,
until the tide carries them away.

I am sketching by the river.
I love to sketch frogs, fish, and even water bugs. I notice things I didn't notice before.
Do they notice **me** ?

I am viewing the world through a camera lens.
I compose **curious** photographs of my friends.

When I carve it's like
the stone is telling me stories.
My tools and hands listen.

I made a collage of
things that I love,
Tied with strings
to the ceiling above.

I am colouring outside the lines.

Instead of mistakes,
I think I make surpises.

I am weaving a basket
while my sister sleeps.

My mother showed me how,
and one day my sister will learn too.
My favourite thread is blue.

I am creating with
my stick in the sand.
It curls and twirls,
making marks on the land.

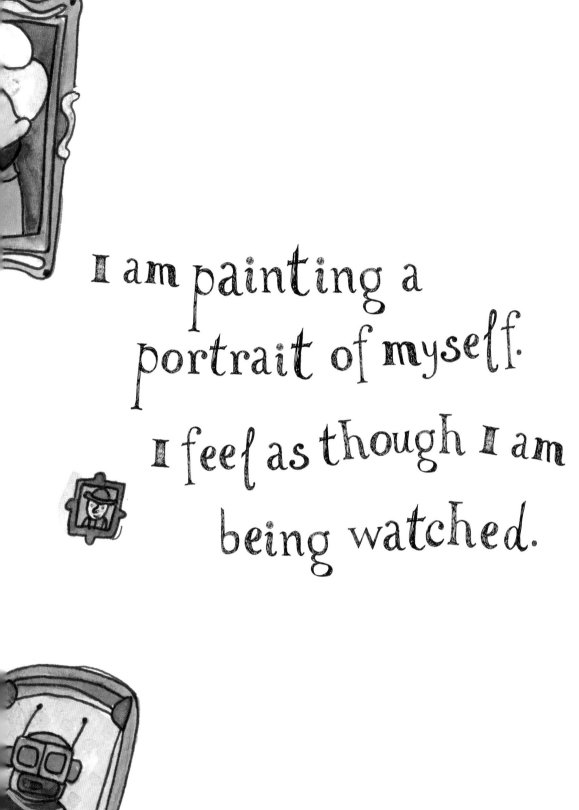

I am painting a portrait of myself.

I feel as though I am being watched.

I am sewing a quilt to keep me warm, while I sit on the hill, watching the storm.

I am drawing a picture from above, as though I were a bird with a pencil flying through alleys and over rooftops.

I am an artist and this
fills me with glee.
You are too, and
always will be.